CHECK-MATE
ISBN 13: 978-1-946467-04-1
ISBN 10: 1-946467-04-9
Copyright © 2019 by Jack Shoup
4514 Briar Hill Rd.
Lexington, KY 40516

Published by:
Piercing Light Publishing
4514 Briar Hill Rd.
Lexington, KY 40516
502-570-9343
Printed in the United States of America.
All rights reserved under International Copyright Law. Contents and/or cover may not be reproduced in whole or in part in any form without the express written consent of the Publisher.

Cover Design by Troy D. Ledford at bluewhaleinnovation.com

CHECK-MATE

by
Jack Shoup

TABLE OF CONTENTS

	Page
Acknowledgments	1
Section 1: **The Goal**	3
Section 2: **Marital Priority**	7
Section 3: **Who is Your Spouse?**	9
Section 4: **Dreams and Desires**	13
Section 5: **Communication**	15
Section 6: **Church**	17
Section 7: **Finances**	19
Section 8: **Workload at Home**	21
Section 9: **Intimacy**	23
Section 10: **Covenant Maintenance**	25
Section 11: **Conflict Resolution**	27
Section 12: **Marriage Confessions**	29
Section 13: **Journaling Your Efforts**	31
About the Author	33

Acknowledgments

Thank you to my wife, Patty, who has put up with me as I have attempted to learn and apply the principles discussed in this book.

Thank you to Tammy Caldararo, Billie Jean Miller, and Jayna Struck for their well thought-out inputs that aided me in assembling the contents of this book.

Jack Shoup

CHECK-MATE

A Study Guide & Workbook to Provide Enhanced Knowledge of your Spouse

THE GOAL

Ephesians 5:31 – For this cause shall a man leave his father and mother, and shall be joined unto his wife, and they two shall become one flesh.

Please understand that this is not a marriage manual specifically designed to restore your broken marriage, however, in some cases it may do so. This is a study guide to help you to enhance the marriage that you and your spouse both want to see rise to higher levels. The gist of this workbook is to initiate a lifestyle that includes a habitual study of your mate. As well, this workbook is not meant to provide you with ammunition to criticize your mate but rather to discover avenues with which to bless them.

Whom we love, we study, research, and speak of incessantly. If we are enamored with sports, we read all that we can get our hands on that discusses our favorite teams. If hooked on fishing, we do likewise. Cooking, fashion, and crafts can all fall into the same category. For the Christian, who has genuinely expressed a love for their savior Jesus, their intense level of study to know God will last their entire life.

However, many who have professed a great love for their spouse often spend little extended effort on studying their mate. The first question we must ask ourselves is, "How much focus do we place on studying and even interviewing our mate?" We are complex beings with numerous likes, dislikes, and habits that make each of us unique. Just as it is somewhat impossible to solve a Rubik's Cube when blindfolded (without having seen what it looked like before the blindfold was put in place), it is also impossible to produce a near perfect marriage without taking time to do an in-depth study of your spouse. God placed in the Old Testament law the need for newlywed couples to take time to get to know each other apart from the worlds distractions.

Deuteronomy 24:5 – When a man hath taken a new wife, he shall not go out to war, neither shall he be charged with any business: but he shall be free at home one year, and shall cheer up his wife which he hath taken.

    This workbook is designed to aid you in beginning, not merely a year, but a lifestyle of spouse-study. The goal of this is to produce the maximum level of marital unity and harmony possible. Marriage should not be based upon a personal decision to merely co-exist. Marriage should involve a joint effort to bring one another's dreams, desires, and callings into manifestation. Such diverse goals cannot possibly be reached without knowledge of what they might be. Included in this study guide are a series of questions which will cause you to reflect upon the needs and desires your mate hopes to see fulfilled in their life.

    This guide is a private book between you and God. In completing this survey, no one is going to check your answers or monitor your efforts. However, should you and your spouse desire to work together jointly and share your answers, feel free to do so.

    The study of your spouse should be established as a life-long endeavor. Therefore, no workbook can ask all of the questions necessary to produce a blessed union. The questions included are provided to set forth a starting point to begin this greatly rewarding pursuit of knowledge.

    With some of the questions, it may may be necessary that you interview your spouse to assure you get the correct answers. For some of the questions, the answer space is split into two parts. This is designed to allow you to guess your spouse's response and then later fill in their actual answer – should you choose to interview them. Perhaps you will be surprised with several of your mate's answers.

    When interviewing your partner, to receive honest and even

intimate answers, it is vital that they know you will not violate their trust and privacy. Any answers must stay between you and your mate.

Another final note before you begin, when interviewing your spouse, assure they are willing to answer what they really feel versus what they think that you desire to hear. We need to hear the truth if we really want to hit the bullseye in producing a great marriage.

We will begin with some relatively easy questions and progress from there. Are you ready to begin?

MARITAL PRIORITY

Ephesians 5:25 – Husbands, love your wives, even as Christ also loved the church, and gave himself for it;

How important is your marriage to you? _____

Why? _____
_____

Do you believe that your marriage can be enhanced? Yes or No

Circle each of the following that are more important to you than your spouse?   Television   Internet   Social Media   Hobbies   Sports   Pets   Relatives   Friends   Children   None of these.

Do you value a great marriage enough to invest sufficient time to make it better?   Yes or No

Do you value a great marriage enough to invest significant effort to make it better? Yes or No

Are you willing to be found wrong and even admit it? Yes or No

Are you willing to change? Yes or No*

> * If you answered no to the above question, please give this workbook to someone who really DOES want to have a better marriage .

WHO IS YOUR SPOUSE?

1Peter 3:7 – Likewise, ye husbands, dwell with them according to knowledge, giving honor unto the wife...

What is your spouse's favorite: The 1st space is for your guess. The 2nd space is for their answer.

Food? _____ _____
Color? _____ _____
Song? _____ _____
Season? _____ _____
Movie? _____ _____
Hobby? _____ _____
Recreation? _____ _____
Reading Material? _____ _____
Automobile? _____ _____
Time of Day? _____ _____
Chocolate/Dessert? _____ _____
Household Temp? _____ _____
Perfume/ Cologne? _____ _____
Gold or Silver? _____ _____
Pizza Toppings? _____ _____
Cornbread/Biscuits? _____ _____
Fruit _____ _____
Back Rubs or Foot Massage? _____ _____
Day or Event in their life? _____
_____

For each of these, what do they dislike?
Food? _____ _____
Song? _____ _____
Season? _____ _____
Movie? _____ _____
Recreation? _____ _____
Reading Material? _____ _____

Time of Day? _____ _____
Chocolate/Dessert? _____ _____
Household Temp? _____ _____
Vegetable? _____ _____

What is their:

Dress/Shirt/Pants size? _____ _____
Ring Size? ____ ____   Eye Color? _____ _____
Shoe size? ____ ____   Birth City? _____ _____
Birth Stone? _____ _____
First Car? _____ _____
What is their earliest memory? _____
_____

Favorite genres of:
- Movie? (comedy, drama, etc) _____
  _____
- Music? _____
  _____

Who were your spouse's best friends when growing up? _____
_____
How many first cousins does your spouse have? _____
What is the worst trouble that your spouse ever got into? _____
_____
Does your spouse eat off of your plate? Yes or No
Does your spouse fuss at you while you are driving? Yes or No
What are your spouse's greatest fears? _____
_____

    The scriptures list seven "Motivational Gifts" in Romans Chapter 8.[1] They are:
    * Prophecy * Serving * Teaching * Exhortation
        * Giving * Facilitation * Mercy

[1] A valuable book to read on this topic is **Discover Your God-Given Gifts** by Dan & Katie Fortune.

Which of these do you believe is your spouse's primary motivational gift? _____

Why is it important for you to know this about your spouse?
_____

Do you feel that your spouse is:
Bossy? _____
Opinionated? _____
Flexible? _____
Spontaneous? _____
Easily Angered? _____
Enjoys Speaking Publicly? _____
Hates Sin? _____
Friendly? _____
Excitable? _____
Outspoken? _____
Industrious? _____
Humorous? _____
A Risk Taker? _____
Inquisitive? _____
A Talker/Chatty? _____

DREAMS & DESIRES

Genesis 1:27-28 – So God created man in his own image, in the image of God created he him; male and female created he them. And God blessed them, and God said unto them, Be fruitful, and multiply, and replenish the earth, and subdue it:

What are your mate's favorite activities? _____
_____
Have you tried to honor these in their life and in what fashion?
_____
_____

Are these activities something you can participate in together and are you willing to do so?   Yes   or   No
Can you list any reasons your participation might be beneficial to your marriage? _____
_____

Has your spouse communicated to you what their dreams or desires in life are? ** Yes   or   No

What is their dream:
Vacation? _____ _____
Automobile? _____ _____
Place to Live? _____ _____
Home Attributes? _____

Job/Career? _____ _____
Possession? _____ _____
Financial Level? _____ _____
Family Structure? _____ _____
Relationships Restored? _____ _____
Personal Changes? _____ _____

** The subject of divine callings will be covered in the section regarding "Church."

Has your spouse ever demonstrated any frustration over unfulfilled dreams? Yes or No
If so, Which ones? _____

Are your dreams important to you? Yes or No

Is it conceivable that your spouse's dreams are equally important to them? Yes or No

What would be the effect upon your spouse and your marriage should more of their dreams be fulfilled? _____
_____

Are your spouse's dreams equally a subject of prayer for you as much as your own? Yes or No

Are you willing to take upon yourself their dreams as your own? Yes or No

Have your spouse's dreams been written down? Yes or No
Have these dreams been discussed with you? Yes or No
Have efforts been taken to prioritize these dreams in order of importance? Yes or No
Have plans been developed in an effort to accomplish these dreams? Yes or No
Do you and your spouse take time to review progress toward reaching these dreams? Yes or No
Have you and your spouse assembled an accomplishment list of their dreams which have already been fulfilled? Yes or No

What efforts have you taken to help them reach their attainable dreams? _____

What additional efforts could you take to aid in fulfilling their dreams? _____
_____

COMMUNICATION

Ephesians 4:29 – Let no corrupt communication proceed out of your mouth, but that which is good to the use of edifying, that it may minister grace unto the hearers.

How would you rate the communication level of your marriage on a scale of 1 – 10? _____
What hinders your marriage from having better communications and what can you do to bring improvement? _____
_____
_____

How do you speak to your spouse? In anger, frustration, critically, or pleasant and edifying? _____
Is your spouse afraid to approach you on certain topics for fear that you may become angered? Yes or No
How would you like to be married to you and why or why not?
_____
_____

Are you interested in what goes on in your spouse's life? Yes or No
Do you want to know about their days? Yes or No
What subject is your spouse most willing to speak about? _____
_____
Are you willing to listen? Yes or No
Do you set aside time to speak to each other daily? Yes or No
Do you speak at least daily via telephone, etc., when you or your spouse is away from home? Yes or No

Who is more likely to initiate conversations in your home? _____
_____
Does your spouse have to drag information out of you? Yes or No
  - If yes, then why? _____
_____

Can your spouse declare that they need to rest a bit before you converse extensively with them without you being offended?
Yes or No
How much effort do you take to seriously LISTEN to your spouse?
_____

Do you often look your spouse squarely in the eyes while they are speaking? Yes or No

How adept are you at hearing your spouse speak through non-verbal communication? _____

Can you identify when your spouse is:
- Teasing you? _____
- Mocking you? _____
- Listening to you? _____
- Wants to be alone? _____
- Hates what you are doing? _____

Gary Chapman wrote a book titled *The Five Love Languages*. This book lists five different ways people individually express and interpret love. They are:
 * Words of Affirmation * Gift Giving * Quality Time
 * Acts of Service * Physical Touch and Closeness

Through which of these does your spouse primarily express and interpret love? _____
Why is it important to know this? _____
_____

What are some things that you can do daily to express appreciation for your spouse in their love language? _____
_____

What are some ways that your spouse may have expressed appreciation for you in their own love language but possibly not yours? _____

CHURCH

Isaiah 54:5 – For thy Maker is thy husband; the LORD of hosts is his name; ...

Is your spouse saved and serving God?   Yes   or   No
  - If you answered "No" to the above question, do you believe that you can take steps of faith, including manifestation of the power of God's love, to win them to the Kingdom?   Yes   or   No

Are you and your spouse doctrinally in agreement and able to attend the same church? Yes   or   No
  - If you answered "No" to the above question, what steps can you take to continue to develop a good marriage?
_____

Do you support your spouse in their level of church commitment if it exceeds yours?   Yes   or   No
Are you jealous of your spouse's love for God?   Yes   or   No

Do you and your spouse pray and/or study the Bible together at home?   Yes   or   No

Do you preach to your spouse in a condemning fashion if you dislike their actions?   Yes   or   No
  – If so, do they appreciate it?   Yes   or   No
  – Would you be better off trusting God to transform your spouse or should you continue to attempt to change them yourself?   Yes   or   No

Do you know if your spouse has a ministry calling on their life? Yes   or   No
If "Yes," what discussions have the two of you had regarding your joint commitment to the call? _____
_____

Are you willing to support them in this call or are you going to attempt to hinder them in it? _____
_____

Do you encourage your spouse to seek God and pursue the Gifts of the Holy Spirit? Yes or No

What benefits will arise from you supporting your spouse in their pursuit of God? _____
_____

What might be the results of hindering your spouse in their spiritual pursuits? _____
_____

Do you and your spouse encourage one another to consistently attend church services even when neither of you may momentarily feel like doing do? Yes or No

FINANCES

Song of Solomon 8:7 – Many waters cannot quench love, neither can the floods drown it: if a man would give all the substance of his house for love, it would be utterly contemned.

What is your spouse's mindset regarding finances? Are they very conservative and hate to spend money or are they more likely to spend all that they have? _____
What is your own financial mindset? _____
_____

Without going to extremes, what can you do to alleviate any stress upon your spouse from differences in your spending patterns?
_____
_____

Approximately how much cash does your spouse normally carry with them when leaving the house? _____

Does your spouse clip and carry coupons? _____
Does your spouse like to wait for sales before they purchase many items?   Yes   or   No

List some ways your spouse attempts to cut costs when shopping for household purchases. _____
List some ways your spouse attempts to cut costs when shopping for personal needs and desires. _____

In your opinion, does your spouse spend too little or too much on special occasions such as Christmas and Birthdays? _____

Are you willing to allow your spouse to purchase reasonable items that enable them to see their dreams and desires fulfilled? _____

In what ways are you willing to, at times, be extravagant toward your mate? _____
_____

Are you willing to save money toward taking them on a getaway or a dream vacation?   Yes   or   No

Are you willing to reduce your own spending to prevent them from being stressed?   Yes   or   No

Does your spouse attempt to work with you to save funds for emergency purposes? _____

Do you and your spouse keep each other up to date on where money is spent and why?   Yes   or   No
Do both of you keep each other aware of the status of your checking account balance?   Yes   or   No

Do you and your spouse tithe to your local church?   Yes   or   No
If you are not in agreement with tithing, are you willing to allow your spouse to continue tithing regardless?   Yes   or   No

Is your spouse a seed sower who gives to multiple areas of need and opportunity?   Yes   or   No

Within reason, do you cheerfully support them in their giving?
Yes or No

WORKLOAD AT HOME

Ecclesiastes 4:9-10 – Two are better than one; because they have a good reward for their labor. For if they fall, the one will lift up his fellow:

Which chores at home does your spouse enjoy the most? _____
_____
Which chores do they most dislike? _____
_____

Have you discussed with your spouse which tasks are agreed upon to be completed by each? Yes or No
Are you willing to perform tasks at home that you may perceive as being "theirs?" Yes or No
How would your spouse respond if you volunteered to help with some of "their" chores? _____
_____
Can you recognize when your partner is stressed due to workload or household "messes?" Yes or No
What are the signs that indicate that they may feel overwhelmed?
_____
What appropriate steps do you take to relieve the pressure your spouse may be experiencing? _____
_____

Are you willing to:
- _____ Change Diapers?
- _____ Watch the Children?
- _____ Make Beds?
- _____ Take out Trash?
- _____ Do Dishes?
- _____ Do Laundry?
- _____ Wash the Car?
- _____ Mow the Grass?

Do you fuss at your spouse when they attempt to help around the house but they do not complete the tasks to your standards?
Yes   or   No

What effect might this have upon their willingness to help out?
_____

On a 1 – 10 scale where would you rank your spouse with 1 being extremely messy to 10 being OCD neat? _____
Where would you rank yourself? _____
Where would your spouse rank you? _____
Are you willing to bridge some of the gap between the two by altering some of your own housekeeping habits?   Yes   or   No

What chores can you and your spouse enjoy performing together?
_____

Do you encourage your spouse to take a weekly personal rest day from all of their labors?   Yes   or   No
Do they take one?   Yes   or   No

What do they enjoy doing when they take a break from their chores? _____

What are the benefits of your spouse taking a rest day weekly?
_____

Are you willing to perform some additional duties around the house to assure that their rest day is not interrupted?   Yes   or   No

Are both of you able to take rest days simultaneously?   Yes   or   No

On these days, does your spouse desire to do activities with you or would they rather get some time to themselves? _____
Will you honor their decisions without resistance or offense?
Yes   or   No

INTIMACY

Proverbs 5:18-19 – Let thy fountain be blessed: and rejoice with the wife of thy youth. Let her be as the loving hind and pleasant roe; let her breasts satisfy thee at all times; and be thou ravished always with her love.

Does your spouse consider you their best friend? Yes or No
What steps are you taking to make or keep your spouse as your best friend? _____
_____

Does your spouse look forward to spending time alone with you? Yes or No

Do your resist efforts to involve yourself in intimate conversations and actions with others of the opposite sex who are not your spouse? Yes or No

Does your spouse attempt to hold conversations with you that you struggle to make time for? Yes or No

What are the favorite conversational topics of your spouse?
_____
_____

Does your spouse enjoy planning their future with you? Yes or No

Which of your personal attributes does your spouse most appreciate? _____
_____
Which of your personal attributes do they least appreciate?
_____
_____
Which are your spouse's strongest character traits? _____
_____

What are their weaker personal attributes? _____
_____
How do you make an effort to support them in their perceived areas of weakness? _____
_____

Do you make your spouse laugh?   Yes   or   No
Do you cheer for your spouse?   Yes   or   No
Does your spouse feel that you "Have their Back?"   Yes   or   No

Are you willing to openly discuss your fears, desires, and failings intimately with your spouse?   Yes   or   No
Does your spouse feel that they can trust you with any secrets they may reveal to you?   Yes   or   No

Do you and your spouse consider the marriage bed a priority in your relationship?   Yes   or   No
Are you willing to demonstrate interest in the marriage bed and make it a priority yourself?   Yes   or   No
Does your spouse feel that you desire them sexually?   Yes   or   No
Have you fully submitted yourself to meet the sexual needs and even desires of your spouse?   Yes   or   No
Are you willing to recognize, at times, a night when your spouse may not truly be in the mood and not demand further from them? Yes or No
Have you and your spouse discussed what is accepted or enjoyed in the bedroom?   Yes   or   No
Are you agreeable to not take them beyond their own convictions and comfort levels regardless of your own desires?   Yes   or   No
According to your spouse, what are some steps that you might take to enhance your physical relationship with your mate? _____
_____

COVENANT MAINTENANCE

Proverbs 20:6-7 – Most men will proclaim every one his own goodness: but a faithful man who can find? The just man walketh in his integrity: his children are blessed after him.

Covenant Maintenance can be considered as any action, large or small, that strengthens marital bonds and closeness.

How often do you tell your spouse that you love them? _____
_____
Do you express your love for them publicly or do you demean them before others? _____
Does your spouse ever have to question whether you love them or not? Yes or No
What is your spouse's reaction when you surprise them with special acts of affection? _____
_____

Do you or your spouse frequently acknowledge one another's presence through light touches on the hand or arm? Yes or No

Do you and your spouse ever kiss publicly? Yes or No
How often do you and your spouse kiss privately (outside of the bedroom)? _____

What is your spouse's favorite thing that you two can do together on a date? _____

Name four inexpensive activities that you could surprise your spouse with that might have a strong positive impact upon them?
 1. _____
 2. _____
 3. _____
 4. _____

Name two things you could alter in your behaviors that might produce a positive effect on your marriage.
1. _____
2. _____

How frequently do you take time to come up with ways to aid or bless your mate? _____

Does your spouse enjoy it when you massage their neck, back, hands, or feet? Yes or No
Would your spouse be appreciative if you increased the frequency of any or all of the above? Yes or No

What "Special Occasions" does your spouse believe merit "special attention" or gifts from you? _____
_____

What verses of Scripture do you routinely speak over your marriage? _____

CONFLICT RESOLUTION

Ephesians 4:26 – Be ye angry, and sin not: let not the sun go down upon your wrath:

Are you willing to overlook your spouse's errors and shortcomings? Yes or No
How does your spouse respond to disagreement? _____
_____
How does your spouse react when you reflect displeasure with them? _____
_____
How do you know when your spouse is upset with you? _____
_____

Is it important to your spouse that they "win" in any argument or disagreement? Yes or No
Is it important to you to "win?"   Yes or No
Do you always have to be "right?"   Yes or No

Are you willing to apologize when you find that you are wrong in a disagreement? Yes or No
Are you willing to apologize even if you believe that you are "right" in a disagreement? Yes or No

How quick are you to forgive your spouse when they apologize?
_____
How quick are you to forgive your spouse when they don't apologize? _____

What actions could you take to assure that your mate feels safe and secure in your marriage even when you disagree? _____
_____
Do you refuse attempts to use manipulation (exaggerated tears, shouting, silent treatment, or abstinence) upon your spouse when you disagree? Yes or No

27

Which of the following "Rules of Engagement" have you and your spouse implemented when in disagreement:
- ____ No name calling
- ____ No declaring "You always"
- ____ No bringing up the past
- ____ No comparison to someone else (especially a parent)
- ____ No mental records of past disappointments are kept
- ____ Maintained respect

When in a disagreement, would your spouse state that you:
- ____ Abandon or avoid the issue and hope it goes away?
- ____ Argue your point until the end?
- ____ Go off and sulk?
- ____ Threaten to leave?
- ____ Attempt to openly discuss the issues to reach a compromised agreement?
- ____ Demonstrate genuine love and commitment for them regardless of the differences?

Who in your marriage is most likely to act as the peacemaker in the midst of strife? _____

In order to remove strife and aid your spouse in overcoming any division or hurt, what steps or actions could you take to act as a peacemaker? _____

_____

MARRIAGE CONFESSIONS

Proverbs 18:21 – Death and life are in the power of the tongue: and they that love it shall eat the fruit thereof.

      One of the most powerful tools that the Christian possesses is to speak God's Word over their life. Included below are some Bible verses that you can speak over your marriage. They have been slightly reworded to make them more personal to you.
      Please consider selecting a few of these and faithfully confessing them over you and your mate. As you do so, it has the potential to release the power of God into your marriage to accomplish what you cannot do of yourself.

Genesis 2:24 –
Therefore, as my spouse and I have left our fathers and mothers, we cleave to one another.

Ephesians 5:25 –
Husband: *I love my wife as Christ also loved the church and gave himself for it.*
Wife: *My Husband loves me as Christ also loved the church and gave himself for it.*

Psalm 128:3 -
Husband: *My wife is as a fruitful vine within our house: my children are like olive plants around our table.*
Wife: *I am as a fruitful vine within our house: my children are like olive plants around our table.*

Ephesians 5:33 -
Husband: *I love my wife just as I love myself; and my wife reverences me as her husband.*
Wife: *My husband loves me just as he loves himself; and I equally reverence my husband.*

Proverbs 18:22 -
Husband: *When I found my wife I found a good thing and obtained favor of the LORD.*
Wife: *When my husband found me he found a good thing and obtained favor of the LORD.*

Proverbs 19:14 -
Husband: *Houses and riches are the inheritance of fathers: and my prudent wife is from the LORD.*
Wife: *Houses and riches are the inheritance of fathers: and I, as a prudent wife, am a gift to my husband from the LORD.*

Proverbs 31:10 -
Husband: *I have found a virtuous woman! For her value is far above rubies.*
Wife: *My husband has found a virtuous woman! For my value is far above rubies.*

JOURNALING YOUR EFFORTS

Habakkuk 2:2 – And the LORD answered me and said, Write the vision, and make it plain upon tables, that he may run that readeth it.

The purpose of this workbook is to initiate in you a new mindset which produces for you an altered lifestyle. This new lifestyle incorporates a continual study of your spouse to better understand and meet their needs. One of the best tools that you can use to aid you in doing this is to journal your efforts and results.

As you endeavor to shift your own personal actions and attitudes regarding your marriage, you can track what seems to be appreciated by your spouse. Be sure to record what seems to have a significant and even lasting impact upon your marriage. This journaling is not to keep score or to track your mate's shortcomings but to help you in being a better spouse.

This study guide does not provide sufficient pages or space to maintain a sufficient record of your efforts. You may want to purchase a dated journal with adequate space to keep your records. The purpose of this section is to provide some ideas of what might be included in your new personal journal. Here are some questions that you might ask yourself regarding what information you want to record or targets you may want to establish:

Over the Next Year -

How often do you want to tell your spouse that you love them?

How often do you want to go out of your way to bless your spouse?

What daily actions do you plan to take to be a blessing to your mate?

What special plans do you want to make with your spouse?

How often will you set aside time to interview or just study your spouse?

What new positive attributes have you noticed in your spouse as a result of your efforts?

What personal changes has your spouse made or experienced this year?

What daily observations of your spouse do you desire to journal?

Do you want to journal "significant events" in your spouse's life for later reference?

How is your spouse responding to your increased attention to them?

Has your increased focus on your marriage been worth the effort?

     I hope this workbook/study guide proves to be a blessing to you. If so, drop me a line through the contact information listed at the rear of this book.

Be Blessed
Pastor Jack Shoup

About the Author

Jack Shoup is founder and senior pastor of Grace Fellowship of Georgetown located in Georgetown, Kentucky.

He is a graduate of The University of Tennessee in mechanical engineering and has an MBA from Xavier University. Beginning in 1977, Jack spent 14 years with IBM Corp. and another 2 years with Lexmark Corp. working in both engineering, business office, and management positions.

Jack and his wife Patty were both saved the same evening soon after they were wed in 1984. From that moment, Jack was imparted an insatiable hunger for the Word of God. He was called into full-time ministry in 1993 and has served as Pastor of Outreach Ministries, as an Assistant Pastor, and since 2001, as a senior pastor.

Jack is called of God to search out the Scriptures and to impart, through his teaching, in-depth understanding of the spiritual principles that govern the Kingdom of God. His primary area of instruction has focused much on the love of God and on the covenant that believer's enter into as members of the Body of Christ.

Jack and Patty have two daughters, Amy and Lori, both grown and pursuing their own careers.

Contact Information

Pastor Jack Shoup may be contacted via the following:

Grace Fellowship of Georgetown
401 Outlet Center Dr
Georgetown, Kentucky 40324

gracegtn@gracegeorgetown.org

(502)570-9343

www.ingramcontent.com/pod-product-compliance
Lightning Source LLC
Chambersburg PA
CBHW052209110526
44591CB00012B/2149